I ♥ Logs

Jay Kreps

Beijing · Cambridge · Farnham · Köln · Sebastopol · Tokyo

I ♥ Logs

by Jay Kreps

Published by O'Reilly Media, Inc., 1005 Gravenstein Highway North, Sebastopol, CA 95472.

O'Reilly books may be purchased for educational, business, or sales promotional use. Online editions are also available for most titles (*http://safaribooksonline.com*). For more information, contact our corporate/institutional sales department: 800-998-9938 or *corporate@oreilly.com*.

Editor: Mike Loukides	**Proofreader:** Eliahu Sussman
Production Editor: Nicole Shelby	**Interior Designer:** David Futato
Copyeditor: Sonia Saruba	**Cover Designer:** Ellie Volckhausen
	Illustrator: Rebecca Demarest

October 2014:   First Edition

Revision History for the First Edition
2014-09-22:   First Release

See *http://oreilly.com/catalog/errata.csp?isbn=9781491909386* for release details.

978-1-491-90938-6

[LSI]

Table of Contents

Preface

Conventions Used in This Book

The following typographical conventions are used in this book:

Italic

> Indicates new terms, URLs, email addresses, filenames, and file extensions.

`Constant width`

> Used for program listings, as well as within paragraphs to refer to program elements such as variable or function names, databases, data types, environment variables, statements, and keywords.

Safari® Books Online

Safari Books Online is an on-demand digital library that delivers expert content in both book and video form from the world's leading authors in technology and business.

Technology professionals, software developers, web designers, and business and creative professionals use Safari Books Online as their primary resource for research, problem solving, learning, and certification training.

Safari Books Online offers a range of plans and pricing for enterprise, government, education, and individuals.

Members have access to thousands of books, training videos, and prepublication manuscripts in one fully searchable database from publishers like O'Reilly Media, Prentice Hall Professional, Addison-Wesley Professional, Microsoft Press, Sams, Que, Peachpit Press, Focal Press, Cisco Press, John Wiley & Sons, Syngress, Morgan Kaufmann, IBM Redbooks, Packt, Adobe Press, FT Press, Apress, Manning, New Riders, McGraw-Hill, Jones & Bartlett, Course Technology, and hundreds more. For more information about Safari Books Online, please visit us online.

How to Contact Us

Please address comments and questions concerning this book to the publisher:

O'Reilly Media, Inc.
1005 Gravenstein Highway North
Sebastopol, CA 95472
800-998-9938 (in the United States or Canada)
707-829-0515 (international or local)
707-829-0104 (fax)

We have a web page for this book, where we list errata, examples, and any additional information. You can access this page at *http://bit.ly/i_heart_logs*.

To comment or ask technical questions about this book, send email to *bookquestions@oreilly.com*.

For more information about our books, courses, conferences, and news, see our website at *http://www.oreilly.com*.

Find us on Facebook: *http://facebook.com/oreilly*

Follow us on Twitter: *http://twitter.com/oreillymedia*

Watch us on YouTube: *http://www.youtube.com/oreillymedia*

CHAPTER 1

Introduction

This is a book about logs. Why would someone write so much about logs? It turns out that the humble log is an abstraction that is at the heart of a diverse set of systems, from NoSQL databases to cryptocurrencies. Yet other than perhaps occasionally tailing a log file, most engineers don't think much about logs. To help remedy that, I'll give an overview of how logs work in distributed systems, and then give some practical applications of these concepts to a variety of common uses: data integration, enterprise architecture, real-time data processing, and data system design. I'll also talk about my experiences putting some of these ideas into practice in my own work on data infrastructure systems at LinkedIn. But to start with, I should explain something you probably think you already know.

What Is a Log?

When most people think about logs they probably think about something that looks like Figure 1-1.

Every programmer is familiar with this kind of log—a series of loosely structured requests, errors, or other messages in a sequence of rotating text files.

This type of log is a degenerative form of the log concept I am going to describe. The biggest difference is that this type of application log is mostly meant for humans to read, whereas the logs I'll be describing are also for programmatic access.

Actually, if you think about it, the idea of humans reading through logs on individual machines is something of an anachronism. This approach quickly becomes unmanageable when many services and servers are involved. The purpose of logs quickly becomes an input to queries and graphs in order to understand behavior across many machines, something that English text in files is not nearly as appropriate for as the kind of structured log I'll be talking about.

```
jkreps-mn:~ jkreps$ tail -f -n 20 /var/log/apache2/access_log
::1 - - [23/Mar/2014:15:07:00 -0700] "GET /images/apache_feather.gif HTTP/1.1" 200 4128
::1 - - [23/Mar/2014:15:07:04 -0700] "GET /images/producer_consumer.png HTTP/1.1" 200 86
::1 - - [23/Mar/2014:15:07:04 -0700] "GET /images/log_anatomy.png HTTP/1.1" 200 19579
::1 - - [23/Mar/2014:15:07:04 -0700] "GET /images/consumer-groups.png HTTP/1.1" 200 268:
::1 - - [23/Mar/2014:15:07:04 -0700] "GET /images/log_compaction.png HTTP/1.1" 200 41414
::1 - - [23/Mar/2014:15:07:04 -0700] "GET /documentation.html HTTP/1.1" 200 189893
::1 - - [23/Mar/2014:15:07:04 -0700] "GET /images/log_cleaner_anatomy.png HTTP/1.1" 200
::1 - - [23/Mar/2014:15:07:04 -0700] "GET /images/kafka_log.png HTTP/1.1" 200 134321
::1 - - [23/Mar/2014:15:07:04 -0700] "GET /images/mirror-maker.png HTTP/1.1" 200 17054
::1 - - [23/Mar/2014:15:08:07 -0700] "GET /documentation.html HTTP/1.1" 200 189937
::1 - - [23/Mar/2014:15:08:07 -0700] "GET /styles.css HTTP/1.1" 304 -
::1 - - [23/Mar/2014:15:08:07 -0700] "GET /images/kafka_logo.png HTTP/1.1" 304 -
::1 - - [23/Mar/2014:15:08:07 -0700] "GET /images/producer_consumer.png HTTP/1.1" 304 -
::1 - - [23/Mar/2014:15:08:07 -0700] "GET /images/log_anatomy.png HTTP/1.1" 304 -
::1 - - [23/Mar/2014:15:08:07 -0700] "GET /images/consumer-groups.png HTTP/1.1" 304 -
::1 - - [23/Mar/2014:15:08:07 -0700] "GET /images/log_cleaner_anatomy.png HTTP/1.1" 304
::1 - - [23/Mar/2014:15:08:07 -0700] "GET /images/log_compaction.png HTTP/1.1" 304 -
::1 - - [23/Mar/2014:15:08:07 -0700] "GET /images/kafka_log.png HTTP/1.1" 304 -
::1 - - [23/Mar/2014:15:08:07 -0700] "GET /images/mirror-maker.png HTTP/1.1" 304 -
::1 - - [23/Mar/2014:15:09:55 -0700] "GET /documentation.html HTTP/1.1" 200 195264
```

Figure 1-1. An excerpt from an Apache log

The log I'll be discussing is a little more general and closer to what in the database or systems world might be called a *commit log* or *journal*. It is an append-only sequence of records ordered by time, as in Figure 1-2.

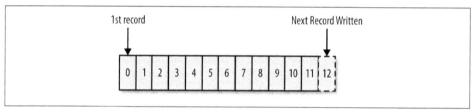

Figure 1-2. A structured log (records are numbered beginning with 0 based on the order in which they are written)

Each rectangle represents a record that was appended to the log. Records are stored in the order they were appended. Reads proceed from left to right. Each entry appended to the log is assigned a unique, sequential log entry number that acts as its unique key. The contents and format of the records aren't important for the purposes of this discussion. To be concrete, we can just imagine each record to be a JSON blob, but of course any data format will do.

The ordering of records defines a notion of "time" since entries to the left are defined to be older then entries to the right. The log entry number can be thought of as the "timestamp" of the entry. Describing this ordering as a notion of time seems a bit odd at first, but it has the convenient property of being decoupled from any particular physical clock. This property will turn out to be essential as we get to distributed systems.

A log is not all that different from a file or a table. A file is an array of bytes, a table is an array of records, and a log is really just a kind of table or file where the records are sorted by time.

You can see the analogy to the Apache log I showed earlier: both are append-only sequences of records. However, it is important that we think about the log as an abstract data structure, not a text file.

At this point you might be wondering, "Why is it worth talking about something so simple?" How is an append-only sequence of records in any way related to data systems? The answer is that logs have a specific purpose: they record what happened and when. For distributed data systems this is, in many ways, the very heart of the problem.

Logs in Databases

I don't know where the log concept originated—it is probably one of those things like binary search that is too simple for the inventor to realize it was an invention. It is present as early as IBM's System R (*http://bit.ly/system-r*). The usage in databases has to do with keeping in sync a variety of data structures and indexes in the presence of crashes. To make this atomic and durable, a database uses a log to write out information about the records it will be modifying before applying the changes to all the various data structures that it maintains. The log is the record of what happened, and each table or index is a projection of this history into some useful data structure or index. Since the log is immediately persisted, it is used as the authoritative source in restoring all other persistent structures in the event of a crash.

Over time, the usage of the log grew from an implementation detail of the ACID database properties (atomicity, consistency, isolation, and durability) to a method for replicating data between databases. It turns out that the sequence of changes that happened on the database is exactly what is needed to keep a remote replica database in sync. Oracle, MySQL, PostgreSQL, and MongoDB include log shipping protocols to transmit portions of a log to replica databases that act as slaves. The slaves can then apply the changes recorded in the log to their own local data structures to stay in sync with the master. Oracle has productized the log as a general data subscription mechanism for non-Oracle data subscribers with their XStreams (*http://bit.ly/xstreams*) and GoldenGate (*http://bit.ly/g-gate*) products, and similar facilities exist in MySQL and PostgreSQL.

In fact, the use of logs in much of the rest of this book will be variations on the two uses in database internals:

1. The log is used as a publish/subscribe mechanism to transmit data to other replicas

---

2. The log is used as a consistency mechanism to order the updates that are applied to multiple replicas

Somehow, perhaps because of this origin in database internals, the concept of a machine readable log is not widely known, although, as we will see, this abstraction is ideal for supporting all kinds of messaging, data flow, and real-time data processing.

Logs in Distributed Systems

The same problems that databases solve with logs (like distributing data to replicas and agreeing on update order) are among the most fundamental problems for all distributed systems.

The log-centric approach to distributed systems arises from a simple observation that I will call the state machine replication principle:

> If two identical, deterministic processes begin in the same state and get the same inputs in the same order, they will produce the same output and end in the same state.

This may seem a bit obtuse, so let's dive in and understand what it means.

Deterministic means that the processing isn't timing dependent and doesn't let any other out-of-band input influence its results. For example, the following can be modeled as nondeterministic: a multithreaded program whose output depends on the order of execution of threads, or a program that makes decisions based on the results of a call to gettimeofday(), or some other non-repeatable source of input. Of course, whether these things are in fact truly deterministic is more a question about the foundations of physics. However, for our purposes it is fine that we don't know enough about their state and inputs to model their output as a proper mathematical function.

The *state* of the process is whatever data remains on the machine, either in memory or on disk, after our processing.

The part about getting the same input in the same order should ring a bell—that is where the log comes in.

So this is actually a very intuitive notion: if you feed two deterministic pieces of code the same input log, they will produce the same output in the same order.

The application to distributed computing is pretty obvious. You can reduce the problem of making multiple machines all do the same thing to the problem of implementing a consistent log to feed input to these processes. The purpose of the log here is to squeeze all the nondeterminism out of the input stream to ensure that each replica that is processing this input stays in sync.

Once you understand it, there is nothing complicated or deep about this principle: it simply amounts to saying "deterministic processing is deterministic." Nevertheless, I think it is one of the more general tools for distributed systems design.

Nor is there anything new about this. If distributed computing is old enough to have a classical approach, this would be it.

However, the implications of this basic design pattern are not that widely appreciated, and the applications to enterprise architecture are appreciated even less.

One of the beautiful things about this is that the discrete log entry numbers now act as a clock for the state of the replicas—you can describe the state of each replica by a single number: the timestamp for the maximum log entry that it has processed. Two replicas at the same time will be in the same state. Thus, this timestamp combined with the log uniquely capture the entire state of the replica. This gives a discrete, event-driven notion of time that, unlike the machine's local clocks, is easily comparable between different machines.

Variety of Log-Centric Designs

There are many variations on how this principle can be applied, depending on what is put in the log. For example, we can log the incoming requests to a service and have each replica process these independently. Or we can have one instance process requests and log the state changes that the service undergoes in response to a request. Theoretically, we could even log a series of x86 machine instructions for each replica to execute, or the method name and arguments to invoke on each replica. As long as two processes handle these inputs in the same way, the processes will remain consistent across replicas.

Different communities describe similar patterns differently. Database people generally differentiate between *physical* and *logical* logging. Physical or row-based logging means logging the contents of each row that is changed. Logical or statement logging means not logging the changed rows, but instead logging the SQL commands that lead to the row changes (the insert, update, and delete statements).

The distributed systems literature commonly distinguishes two broad approaches to processing and replication. The *state machine model* usually refers to an active-active model, where we keep a log of the incoming requests and each replica processes each request in log order. A slight modification of this, called the *primary-backup model*, is to elect one replica as the leader. This leader processes requests in the order they arrive and logs the changes to its state that occur as a result of processing the requests. The other replicas apply the state changes that the leader makes so that they will be in sync and ready to take over as leader, should the leader fail.

As shown in Figure 1-3, in the primary backup model a master node is chosen to handle all reads and writes. Each write is posted to the log. Slaves subscribe to the log and apply the changes that the master executed to their local state. If the master fails, a new master is chosen from the slaves. In the state machine replication model, all nodes are peers. Writes go first to the log and all nodes apply the write in the order determined by the log.

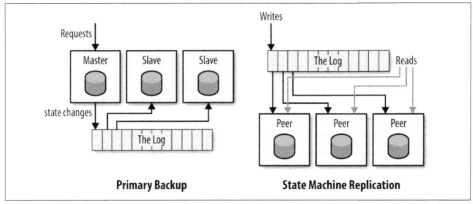

Figure 1-3. In the primary backup model, a master node is chosen to handle all reads and writes. In the state machine replicatio model, all nodes act as peers.

An Example

To understand different approaches to building a system using a log, let's look at a toy problem. Say we want to implement a replicated arithmetic service that maintains a set of variables (initialized to zero) and applies additions, multiplications, subtractions, divisions, and queries on these values. Our service will respond to the following commands:

```
x? // get the current value of x
x+=5 // add 5 to x
x-=2 // subtract 2 from x
y*=2 // double y
```

Let's say that this is run as a remote web service, with requests and responses sent via HTTP.

If we have only a single server, the implementation will be quite simple. It can store the variables in memory or on disk and update them in whatever order it happens to receive requests. However, because there is only a single server, we lack fault tolerance and also have no way to scale out serving (should our arithmetic service become popular).

We can solve this by adding servers that replicate this state and processing logic. However this creates a new problem: the servers might get out of sync. There are many ways this could happen. For example, the servers could receive the update commands in different orders (not all operations are commutative), or a failed or nonresponsive server could miss updates.

Of course, in practice, most people would just push the queries and updates into a remote database. This moves the problem out of our application, but doesn't really solve it; after all, now we need to solve the fault tolerance problem in the database. So for the sake of the example, let's directly discuss the use of a log in our application.

There are a few variations on solving this problem using a log. The state-machine replication approach would involve first writing to the log the operation that is to be performed, then having each replica apply the operations in the log order. In this case, the log would contain a sequence of commands like "x+=5" or "y*=2".

A primary-backup approach is also possible. In this design, we would choose one of the replicas to act as the primary (or leader or master). This primary would locally execute whatever command it receives in the order requests arrive, and it would log out the series of variable values that result from executing the commands. In this design, the log contains only the resulting variable values, like "x=1" or "y=6", not the original commands that created the values. The remaining replicas would act as back-ups (or followers or slaves); they subscribe to this log and passively apply the new variable values to their local stores. When the leader fails, we would choose a new leader from among the remaining replicas.

This example also makes it clear why ordering is key for ensuring consistency between replicas: reordering an addition and multiplication command will yield a different result, as will reordering two variable updates for the same variable.

Logs and Consensus

The distributed log can be seen as the data structure that models the problem of consensus. A log, after all, represents a series of decisions on the next value to append. You have to squint a little to see a log in the Paxos family of algorithms, although log building is their most common practical application. With Paxos, this is usually done using an extension of the protocol called "multi-paxos," which models the log as a series of consensus problems, one for each slot in the log. The log is much more prominent in other protocols such as ZAB (*http://bit.ly/zab-pro*), RAFT (*http://bit.ly/raft-pro*), and Viewstamped Replication (*http://bit.ly/viewstamped*), which directly model the problem of maintaining a distributed, consistent log.

My suspicion is that our view of this is a little biased by the path of history, perhaps due to the few decades in which the theory of distributed computing outpaced its practical application. In reality, the consensus problem is a bit too simple. Computer systems rarely need to decide a single value, they almost always handle a sequence of requests. So a log, rather than a simple single-value register, is the more natural abstraction.

Furthermore, the focus on the algorithms obscures the underlying log abstraction that systems need. I suspect we will end up focusing more on the log as a commoditized building block irrespective of its implementation in the same way that we often talk about a hash table without bothering to get into the details of whether we mean the murmur hash with linear probing or some other variant. The log will become something of a commoditized interface, with many algorithms and implementations competing to provide the best guarantees and optimal performance.

Changelog 101: Tables and Events Are Dual

Let's come back to databases for a bit. There is a fascinating duality between a log of changes and a table. The log is similar to the list of all credits and debits a bank processes, while a table would be all the current account balances. If you have a log of changes, you can apply these changes in order to create the table and capture the current state. This table will record the latest state for each key (as of a particular log time). There is a sense in which the log is the more fundamental data structure: in addition to creating the original table, you can also transform it to create all kinds of derived tables. (And yes, table can mean keyed data store for you non-relational folks.)

This process works in reverse as well: if you have a table taking updates, you can record these changes and publish a *changelog* of all the updates to the state of the table. This changelog is exactly what you need to support near-real-time replicas. In this sense, you can see tables and events as dual: tables support data at rest and logs capture change. The magic of the log is that if it is a *complete* log of changes, it holds not only the contents of the final version of the table, but can also recreate all other versions that might have existed. It is, effectively, a sort of backup of *every* previous state of the table.

This might remind you of source code version control. There is a close relationship between source control and databases. Version control solves a very similar problem to what distributed data systems have to solve: managing distributed, concurrent changes in state. A version control system usually models the sequence of patches, which is in effect a log. You interact directly with a checked-out snapshot of the current code, which is analogous to the table. Note that in version control systems, as in other distributed stateful systems, replication happens via the log: when you update, you just pull down the patches and apply them to your current snapshot.

Some people have seen some of these ideas recently from Datomic (*http:// www.datomic.com/*), a company selling a log-centric database (*http://bit.ly/log-centric*). These concepts are not unique to this system, of course, as they have been a part of the distributed systems and database literature for well over a decade.

This may all seem a little theoretical. Do not despair! We'll get to the practical stuff quickly.

What's Next

In the remainder of this book, I will give you a flavor of what a log is good for that goes beyond the internals of distributed systems or abstract distributed computing models, including:

Data integration
    Making all of an organization's data easily available in all its storage and processing systems.

Real-time data processing
    Computing derived data streams.

Distributed system design
    How practical systems can by simplified with a log-centric design.

These uses all revolve around the idea of a log as a standalone service.

In each case, the usefulness of the log comes from the simple function that the log provides: producing a persistent, replayable record of history. Surprisingly, at the core of the previously mentioned log uses is the ability to have many machines play back history at their own rates in a deterministic manner.

CHAPTER 2

Data Integration

The first application I want to dive into is data integration. Let me start by explaining what I mean by data integration and why I think it's important, then we'll see how it relates to logs.

> Data integration means making available all the data that an organization has to all the services and systems that need it.

The phrase "data integration" isn't all that common, but I don't know a better one. The more recognizable term ETL (extract, transform, and load) usually covers only a limited part of data integration—populating a relational data warehouse. However, much of what I am describing can be thought of as ETL that is generalized to also encompass real-time systems and processing flows.

You don't hear much about data integration in all the breathless interest and hype around the idea of *big data*; nevertheless, I believe that this mundane problem of making the data available is one of the more valuable goals that an organization can focus on.

Effective use of data follows a kind of Maslow's hierarchy of needs. The base of the pyramid shown in Figure 2-1 involves capturing all the relevant data and being able to put it together in an applicable processing environment (whether a fancy real-time query system or just text files and Python scripts). This data needs to be modeled in a uniform way to make it easy to read and process. Once the basic needs of capturing data in a uniform way are taken care of, it is reasonable to work on infrastructure to process this data in various ways: MapReduce, real-time query systems, and so on.

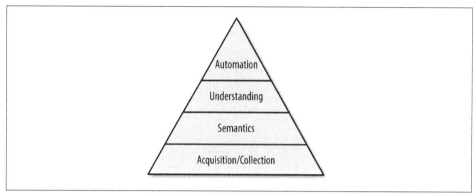

Figure 2-1. A Maslow-like hierarchy for using data. The collection and modeling of data remains a primary concern until these are mastered, then the focus can move to higher level goals.

It's worth noting the obvious: without a reliable and complete data flow, a Hadoop cluster is little more than a very expensive and difficult-to-assemble space heater. Once data and processing are available, you can move on to more refined problems such as good data models and consistent, well understood semantics. Finally, concentration can shift to more sophisticated processing: better visualization, reporting, and algorithmic processing and prediction.

In my experience, most organizations have huge holes in the base of this pyramid— they lack reliable, complete data flow but want to jump directly to deep learning and advanced data modeling techniques. This is completely backwards.

The question is, how can we build reliable data flow throughout all the data systems in an organization?

Data Integration: Two Complications

Two trends have made data integration an increasingly difficult problem.

Data is More Diverse

I think if you asked a company 15 years ago what data they had, they would describe their transactional data, such as users, products, orders, and other items kept in tables in relational databases.

However, our definition has broadened. Now most companies would also include event data. Event data records things that *happen* rather than things that *are*. In web systems, this means user activity logging, as well as the machine-level events and statistics required to reliably operate and monitor a data center's worth of machines. People tend to call this "log data" since it is often written to application logs, but that confuses form with function. This data is at the heart of the modern Web: Google's fortune, after all, is generated by a relevance pipeline built on clicks and impressions —that is, events.

This stuff isn't limited to web companies, it's just that web companies are already fully digital, so they are easier to instrument and measure. Financial data has long been event-centric. RFID adds this kind of tracking to physical objects. I think this trend will continue with the digitization of traditional businesses and activities. The "Internet of Things," though a bit of a buzzword, seeks to describe the trend of connecting physical devices to the digital world. One of the primary motivations for this is to record event data about what these physical devices are doing so we can extend our digital modeling to the physical world and broaden the scope of things that can be programmed and optimized with software.

This type of event data shakes up traditional data integration approaches because it tends to be several orders of magnitude larger than transactional data.

The Explosion of Specialized Data Systems

The second trend is the explosion of specialized data systems (*http://bit.ly/cite-seer*) that have become popular and often freely available in the last five years. Specialized systems exist for OLAP (*http://druid.io/docs/latest/*), search (*http://www.elastic search.org/*), simple (*http://www.rethinkdb.com/*) online (*http://bit.ly/li-ddsp*) storage (*http://cassandra.apache.org/*), batch processing (*http://hadoop.apache.org/*), graph analysis (*http://graphlab.org/*), and so (*http://redis.io/*) on (*http://spark.apache.org/*).

The combination of more data of more varieties and a desire to get this data into more systems leads to a huge data integration problem.

Log-Structured Data Flow

How can we attack this problem? Well, it turns out that the log is the natural data structure for handling data flow between systems. The recipe is very simple:

> Take all of the organization's data and put it into a central log for real-time subscription.

Each logical data source can be modeled as its own log. A data source could be an application that logs events (such as clicks or page views), or a database table that logs modifications. Each subscribing system reads from this log as quickly as it can, applies each new record to its own store, and advances its position in the log. Subscribers could be any kind of data system: a cache, Hadoop, another database in another site, a search system, and so on (see Figure 2-2).

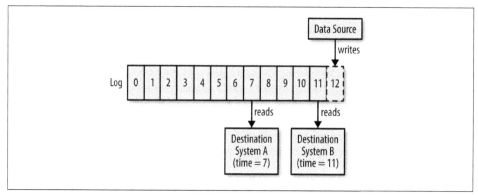

Figure 2-2. A log can be used for publish-subscribe messaging. The publisher appends to the log and each subscriber keeps a pointer to its position in the log, allowing it to read independently.

The log concept gives a logical clock for each change against which all subscribers can be measured. This makes reasoning about the state of the different subscriber systems with respect to one another far simpler, as each has a point in time up to which it has read.

To make this more concrete, consider a simple case where there is a database and a collection of caching servers. The log provides a way to synchronize the updates to all of these systems and reason about their current state based on the point of time they are up to in the log. Let's say we write a record with log entry X and then need to do a read from the cache. If we want to guarantee that we don't see stale data, we just need to ensure that we don't read from any cache that has not replicated up to X.

The log also acts as a buffer that makes data production asynchronous from data consumption. This is important for many reasons, but particularly when there are multiple subscribers that consume at different rates. This means a subscribing system can crash or go down for maintenance and catch up when it comes back up: the subscriber consumes at a pace it controls. A batch system such as Hadoop or a data warehouse might consume only hourly or daily, whereas a real-time query system might need to be up-to-the-second. Neither the originating data source nor the log has knowledge of the various data destination systems, so consumer systems can be added and removed with no change in the pipeline.

Figure 2-3. "Each working data pipeline is designed like a log; each broken data pipeline is broken in its own way." (http://bit.ly/a-karenina)—Count Leo Tolstoy (translation by the author)

Of particular importance: the destination system only knows about the log and does not know any details of the system of origin. The consumer system need not concern itself with whether the data came from a relational database, a new-fangled key-value store, or was generated directly by some application. This seems like a minor point, but is, in fact, critical.

I use the term "log" here instead of "messaging system" or "pub sub" because it is much more specific about semantics and a much closer description of what you need in a practical implementation to support data replication. I have found that "publish subscribe" doesn't imply much more than indirect addressing of messages—if you compare any two messaging systems that both promise publish-subscribe, you find that they guarantee very different things, and most models are not useful in this domain. You can think of the log as acting as a kind of messaging system with durability guarantees and strong ordering semantics. In distributed systems, this model of communication sometimes goes by the (somewhat terrible) name of atomic broadcast.

It's worth emphasizing that the log is still just the infrastructure. This isn't the end of the story of mastering data flow: the rest of the story is around metadata, schemas, compatibility, and the details of handling data structure and evolution. Until there is a reliable, general way of handling the mechanics of data flow, the semantic details are secondary.

My Experience at LinkedIn

I got to watch this data integration problem emerge in fast-forward during my time at LinkedIn as we moved from a centralized relational database to a collection of distributed systems; I'll give an abbreviated history of my experiences with these ideas.

These days, the major data systems LinkedIn runs include:

- Search (*http://bit.ly/li-search*)
- Social graph (*http://bit.ly/s-graph*)
- Voldemort (*http://project-voldemort.com/*) (key-value store)
- Espresso (*http://data.linkedin.com/projects/espresso*) (document store)
- Recommendation engine and ad serving systems (*http://bit.ly/linked-recs*)
- OLAP query engine
- Hadoop (*http://hadoop.apache.org/*)
- Terradata (*http://www.teradata.com/*)
- Ingraphs (*http://bit.ly/ingraphs*) (monitoring graphs and metrics services)
- Newsfeed (the system that serves updates on the home page)

Each of these is a specialized distributed system that provides advanced functionality in its area of specialty.

This idea of using logs for data flow has been floating around LinkedIn since even before I got there. One of the earliest pieces of infrastructure we developed was a service called databus (*http://bit.ly/li-databus*). Databus provided a log caching abstraction on top of our early Oracle tables to scale subscription to database changes so we could feed our social graph and search indexes.

My own involvement in this started around 2008 after we had shipped our key-value store. My next project was to try to get a working Hadoop setup going, and move some of our recommendation processes there. Having little experience in this area, we naturally budgeted a few weeks for getting data in and out, and the rest of our time for implementing fancy prediction algorithms. So began a long slog.

Figure 2-4. ETL in Ancient Greece. (http://bit.ly/etl-greek) Not much has changed.

We originally planned to just scrape the data out of our existing Oracle data warehouse. The first discovery was that getting data out of Oracle quickly is something of a dark art. Worse, the data warehouse processing was not appropriate for the production batch processing we planned for Hadoop—much of the processing was nonreversable and specific to the reporting being done. We ended up avoiding the data warehouse and going directly to source databases and log files. Finally, we implemented another pipeline to load data into our key-value store (*http://bit.ly/li-datacycle*) for serving results.

Each of these pipelines ended up being a significant engineering project. They had to be scaled to run across multiple machines. They had to be monitored, tested, and maintained. This mundane data copying ended up being one of the dominant items in the development we were doing. Worse, anytime there was a problem in one of the pipelines, as there often was in those days, the Hadoop system was largely useless—running fancy algorithms on bad data just produces more bad data.

Although we had built things in a fairly generic way, each new data source required custom configuration to set up. It also proved to be the source of a huge number of errors and failures. The site features we had implemented on Hadoop became popular and we found ourselves with a long list of interested engineers. Each user had a list of systems they wanted integration with and a long list of new data feeds they wanted.

A few things slowly became clear to me.

First, the pipelines we had built, even though a bit of a mess, were actually extremely valuable. Just the process of making data available in a new processing system (Hadoop) unlocked many possibilities. It was possible to do new computation on the data that would have been hard to do before. Many new products and analysis came from simply putting together multiple pieces of data that had previously been locked up in specialized systems.

Second, it was clear that reliable data loads would require deep support from the data pipeline. If we captured all the structure we needed, we could make Hadoop data loads fully automatic, so that no manual effort was expended when adding new data sources or handling schema changes. Data would just magically appear in HDFS, and Hive tables would automatically be generated for new data sources with the appropriate columns.

Third, we still had very low data coverage. That is, if you looked at the overall percentage of the data LinkedIn had that was available in Hadoop, it was still very incomplete. Getting to completion was not going to be easy given the amount of effort required to operationalize each new data source.

The way we had been proceeding—building out custom data loads for each data source and destination—was clearly infeasible. We had dozens of data systems and data repositories. Connecting all of these would have led to building custom piping between each pair of systems, looking something like Figure 2-5.

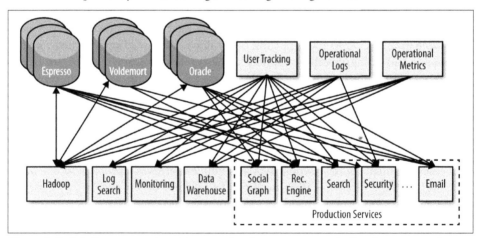

Figure 2-5. A fully connected architecture that has a separate pipeline between each system

Note that data often flows in both directions, as many systems (databases and Hadoop) are both sources and destinations for data transfer. This meant that we would end up building two pipelines per system: one to get data in and one to get data out.

This clearly would take an army of people to build and would never be operable. As we approached full connectivity, we would end up with something like $O(N^2)$ pipelines.

Instead, we needed something generic, as shown in Figure 2-6.

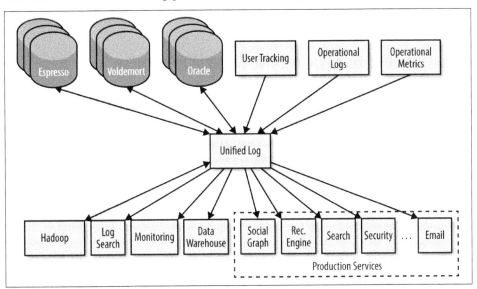

Figure 2-6. An architecture built around a central hub

As much as possible, we needed to isolate each consumer from the source of the data. The consumer should ideally integrate with just a single data repository that would give her access to everything.

The idea is that adding a new data system—be it a data source or a data destination—should create integration work only to connect it to a single pipeline instead of to each consumer of data.

This experience led me to focus on building Kafka (*http://kafka.apache.org/*) to combine what we had seen in messaging systems with the log concept popular in databases and distributed system internals. We wanted something to act as a central pipeline first for all activity data, and eventually for many other uses, including data deployment out of Hadoop, monitoring data, and so on.

For a long time, Kafka was a little unique (some would say odd) as an infrastructure product—neither a database nor a log file collection system nor a traditional messaging system. But recently, Amazon has offered a service that is very similar to Kafka called Kinesis (*http://aws.amazon.com/kinesis*). The similarity goes right down to the way partitioning is handled and data is retained, as well as the fairly odd split in the Kafka API between high- and low-level consumers. I was pretty happy about this. A sign you've created a good infrastructure abstraction is that Amazon offers it as a service! Their vision for this seems to be similar to what I am describing: it is the piping that connects all their distributed systems—DynamoDB, RedShift, S3—as well as the basis for distributed stream processing using EC2. Google has followed with a data stream and processing framework (*http://bit.ly/g-cpb*), and Microsoft has started to move in the same direction with their Azure Service Bus (*http://bit.ly/azure-bus*) offering.

Relationship to ETL and the Data Warehouse

Let's talk data warehousing for a bit. The data warehouse is meant to be a repository for the clean, integrated data structured to support analysis. This is a great idea. For those not in the know, the data warehousing methodology involves periodically extracting data from source databases, munging it into some kind of understandable form, and loading it into a central data warehouse. Having this central location that contains a clean copy of all your data is a hugely valuable asset for data-intensive analysis and processing. At a high level, this methodology doesn't change too much whether you use a traditional data warehouse like Oracle, Teradata, or Hadoop, although you might switch up the order of loading and munging (*http://bit.ly/elt-def*).

A data warehouse containing clean, integrated data is a phenomenal asset, but the mechanics of getting this are a bit out of date.

The key problem for a data-centric organization is coupling the clean integrated data to the data warehouse. A data warehouse is a piece of batch query infrastructure that is well suited to many kinds of reporting and ad hoc analysis, particularly when the queries involve simple counting, aggregation, and filtering. But having a batch system be the only repository of clean, complete data means the data is unavailable for systems requiring a real-time feed: real-time processing, search indexing, monitoring systems, and so on.

ETL is really two things. First, it is an extraction and data cleanup process, essentially liberating data locked up in a variety of systems in the organization and removing any system-specific nonsense. Secondly, that data is restructured for data warehousing queries (that is, made to fit the type system of a relational database, forced into a star or snowflake schema, perhaps broken up into a high performance column (*http://parquet.io/*) format (*http://bit.ly/had-hive*), and so on). Conflating these two roles is a problem. The clean, integrated repository of data should also be available in real time for low-latency processing, and for indexing in other real-time storage systems.

ETL and Organizational Scalability

I think this has the added benefit of making data warehousing ETL much more *organizationally* scalable. The classic problem of the data warehouse team is that they are responsible for collecting and cleaning all the data generated by every other team in the organization. The incentives are not aligned; data producers are often not very aware of the use of the data in the data warehouse and end up creating data that is hard to extract or requires heavy, hard-to-scale transformation to get it into usable form. Of course, the central team never quite manages to scale to match the pace of the rest of the organization, so data coverage is always spotty, data flow is fragile, and changes are slow.

A better approach is to have a central pipeline, the log, with a well-defined API for adding data. The responsibility of integrating with this pipeline and providing a clean, well-structured data feed lies with the producer of this data feed. This means that as part of their system design and implementation, they must consider the problem of getting data out and into a well-structured form for delivery to the central pipeline. The addition of new storage systems is of no consequence to the data warehouse team, as they have a central point of integration. The data warehouse team handles only the simpler problem of loading structured feeds of data from the central log and carrying out transformation specific to their system (see Figure 2-7).

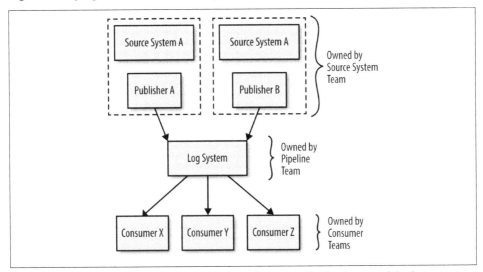

Figure 2-7. There is a human element to data flow as well. This is one of the key aspects of democritizing access to data.

This point about organizational scalability becomes particularly important when an organization considers adopting additional data systems beyond a traditional data warehouse. Say, for example, that you wish to provide search capabilities over the complete data set of the organization. Or, say that you want to provide sub-second monitoring of data streams with real-time trend graphs and alerting. In either case, the infrastructure of the traditional data warehouse or even a Hadoop cluster will be inappropriate. Worse, the ETL processing pipeline built to support database loads is likely of no use for feeding these other systems, making bootstrapping these pieces of infrastructure as large an undertaking as adopting a data warehouse. This likely isn't feasible and probably helps explain why most organizations don't have these capabilities easily available for all their data. By contrast, if the organization had built out feeds of uniform, well-structured data, getting any new system full access to all data requires only a single bit of integration plumbing to attach to the pipeline.

Where Should We Put the Data Transformations?

This architecture also raises a set of different options for where a particular cleanup or transformation can reside:

- It can be done by the data producer prior to adding the data to the company-wide log.
- It can be done as a real-time transformation on the log (which in turn produces a new, transformed log).
- It can be done as part of the load process into some destination data system.

The best model is to have the data publisher do *cleanup* prior to publishing the data to the log. This means ensuring that the data is in a canonical form and doesn't retain any holdovers from the particular code that produced it or the storage system in which it might have been maintained. These details are best handled by the team that creates the data since that team knows the most about its own data. Any logic applied in this stage should be lossless and reversible.

Any kind of value-added transformation that can be done in real-time should be done as post-processing on the raw log feed that was produced. This would include things like sessionization of event data, or the addition of other derived fields that are of general interest. The original log is still available, but this real-time processing produces a derived log containing augmented data.

Finally, only aggregation that is specific to the destination system should be performed as part of the loading process. This might include transforming data into a particular star or snowflake schema for analysis and reporting in a data warehouse. Because this stage, which most naturally maps to the traditional ETL process, is now done on a far cleaner and more uniform set of streams, it should be much simplified.

Decoupling Systems

Let's talk a little bit about a side benefit of this architecture: it enables decoupled, event-driven systems.

The typical approach to activity data in the web industry is to log it out to text files where it can be scrapped into a data warehouse or into Hadoop for aggregation and querying. The problem with this is the same as the problem with all batch ETL: it couples the data flow to the data warehouse's capabilities and processing schedule.

At LinkedIn, we have built our event data handling in a log-centric fashion. We are using Kafka as the central, multisubscriber event log (see Figure 2-8). We have defined several hundred event types, each capturing the unique attributes about a particular type of action. This covers everything from page views, ad impressions, and searches to service invocations and application exceptions.

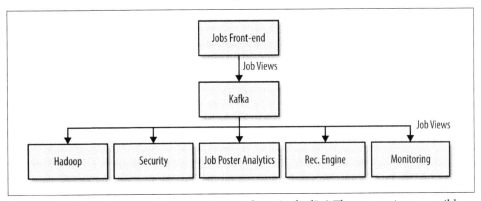

Figure 2-8. What happens when you view a job on LinkedIn? The system is responsible for displaying the job records, and each system that needs to be aware of this subscribes to the stream of all job views and reacts appropriately in its own timeframe.

To understand the advantages of this, imagine a simple event showing a job posting on the job page. The job page should contain only the logic required to display the job. However, in a fairly dynamic site, this could easily become tangled up with additional logic unrelated to showing the job. For example, let's say we need to integrate the following systems:

- We need to send this data to Hadoop and the data warehouse for offline processing purposes.
- A security system needs to count the view to ensure that the viewer is not attempting some kind of content scraping.
- We need to aggregate this view for display in the job poster's analytics page.

- The job recommendation system needs to record the view to ensure that we properly impression cap any job recommendations for that user (we don't want to show the same thing over and over).
- Monitoring systems need to track the display rate and application rate for jobs to ensure that the system is functioning well.

Pretty soon, the simple act of displaying a job has become quite complex. As we add other places where jobs are displayed—mobile applications and so on—this logic must be carried over and the complexity increases. Worse, the systems that we need to interface with are now somewhat intertwined—the person working on displaying jobs needs to know about many other systems and features and make sure they are integrated properly. This is just a toy version of the problem, and any real application would be more complex, not less.

The *event-driven* style provides an approach to simplifying this. The job display page now just shows a job and records the fact that a job was shown along with the relevant attributes of the job, the viewer, and any other useful facts about the display of the job. Each of the other interested systems—the recommendation system, the security system, the job poster analytics system, and the data warehouse—all just subscribe to the feed and do their processing. The display code does not need to be aware of these other systems or changed if a new data consumer is added.

Scaling a Log

Of course, separating publishers from subscribers is nothing new. However, if you want to keep a commit log that acts as a multisubscriber real-time journal of everything happening on a consumer-scale website, scalability will be a primary challenge. Using a log as a universal integration mechanism is never going to be more than an elegant fantasy if we can't build a log that is fast, cheap, and scalable enough to be practical in this domain.

Distributed systems people often think of a distributed log as a slow, heavyweight abstraction (and usually associate it only with the kind of metadata uses for which Zookeeper might be appropriate). With a thoughtful implementation focused on journaling large data streams, this need not be true. As an example, LinkedIn writes hundreds of billions of messages to production Kafka clusters each day.

We used a few tricks in Kafka to support this kind of scale:

- Partitioning the log
- Optimizing throughput by batching reads and writes
- Avoiding needless data copies

In order to allow horizontal scaling, we chop up our log into partitions, as shown in Figure 2-9.

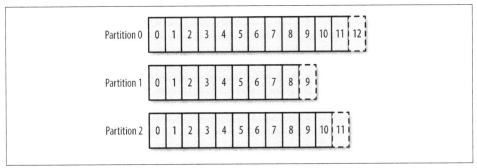

Figure 2-9. By partitioning the log, we allow each partition to act independently of all other partitions. This lets us horizontally scale the write throughput.

Each partition is a totally ordered log, but there is no global ordering between partitions (other than perhaps some wall-clock time you might include in your messages). The writer controls the assignment of the messages to a particular partition, with most users choosing to partition by some kind of key (such as a user ID). Partitioning allows log appends to occur without coordination between shards, and allows the throughput of the system to scale linearly with the Kafka cluster size while still maintaining ordering within the sharding key.

Each partition is replicated across a configurable number of replicas, each of which has an identical copy of the partition's log. At any time, a single partition will act as the leader; if the leader fails, one of the replicas will take over as leader.

Lack of global order across partitions is a limitation, but we have not found it to be a major one. Indeed, interaction with the log typically comes from hundreds or thousands of distinct processes, so it is not meaningful to talk about a total order over their behavior. Instead, the guarantees that we provide are that each partition is order preserving, and Kafka guarantees that appends to a particular partition from a single sender will be delivered in the order they are sent.

A log, like a filesystem, is easy to optimize for linear read and write patterns. The log can group small reads and writes together into larger, high-throughput operations. Kafka pursues this optimization aggressively. Batching occurs from client to server when sending data, in writes to disk, in replication between servers, in data transfer to consumers, and in acknowledging committed data.

Finally, Kafka uses a simple binary format that is maintained between in-memory log, on-disk log, and in-network data transfers. This allows us to make use of numerous optimizations, including zero-copy data transfer (*http://bit.ly/zero-copy*).

The cumulative effect of these optimizations, is that you can usually write and read data at the rate supported by the disk or network, even while maintaining data sets that vastly exceed memory. For example, a single thread can write 100-byte messages at a rate of about 750k messages per second, each being stored with 3x replication. Reading is even faster at about 900k messages per second. More benchmarks are available (*http://bit.ly/apache-k2*).

This write-up isn't meant to be primarily about Kafka so I won't go into further details. You can read a more detailed overview of LinkedIn's approach (*http://bit.ly/li-pipeline*) and a thorough overview of Kafka's design (*http://bit.ly/k-design*).

CHAPTER 3

Logs and Real-Time Stream Processing

So far, I have only described what amounts to a fancy method of copying data from place to place. However, schlepping bytes between storage systems is not the end of the story. It turns out that "log" is another word for "stream" and logs are at the heart of stream processing (*http://bit.ly/stream-pro*).

But wait, what exactly is stream processing?

If you are a fan of database literature or semi-successful data infrastructure products (*http://bit.ly/ibm-streams*) of the late 1990s and early 2000s, you likely associate stream processing with efforts to build a SQL engine or "boxes-and-arrows" interface for event-driven processing.

If you follow the explosion of open source data systems, you likely associate stream processing with some of the systems in this space, for example, Storm (*http://storm.incubator.apache.org/*), Akka (*http://akka.io/*), S4 (*http://incubator.apache.org/s4*), and Samza (*http://samza.incubator.apache.org*). Most people see these as a kind of asynchronous message processing system that is not that different from a cluster-aware RPC layer (and in fact some things in this space are exactly that). I have heard stream processing described as a model where you process all your data immediately and then throw it away.

Both these views are a little limited. Stream processing has nothing to do with SQL. Nor is it limited to real-time processing. There is no inherent reason you can't process the stream of data from yesterday or a month ago using a variety of different languages to express the computation. Nor must you (or should you) throw away the original data that was captured.

I see stream processing as something much broader: infrastructure for continuous data processing. I think the computational model can be as general as MapReduce or other distributed processing frameworks, but with the ability to produce low-latency results.

The real driver for the processing model is the method of data collection. Data collected in batch is naturally processed in batch. When data is collected continuously, it is naturally processed continuously.

The United States census provides a good example of batch data collection. The census periodically kicks off and does a brute force discovery and enumeration of US citizens by having people walk from door to door. This made a lot of sense in 1790 when the census was first begun (see Figure 3-1). Data collection at the time was inherently batch oriented, as it involved riding around on horseback and writing down records on paper, then transporting this batch of records to a central location where humans added up all the counts. These days, when you describe the census process, one immediately wonders why we don't keep a journal of births and deaths and produce population counts either continuously or with whatever granularity is needed.

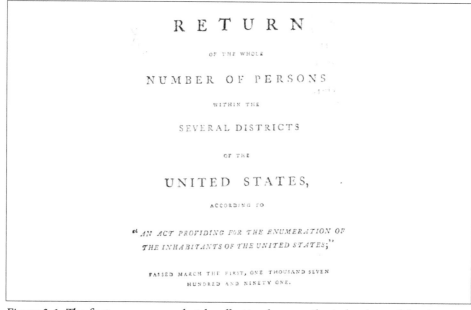

Figure 3-1. The first census was a batch collection because the technology of the time demanded it. However, batch data collection is no longer necessary for a digital, networked organization.

This is an extreme example, but many data transfer processes still depend on taking periodic dumps and bulk transfer and integration. The only natural way to process a bulk dump is with a batch process. As these processes are replaced with continuous feeds, we naturally start to move towards continuous processing to smooth out the processing resources needed and reduce latency.

A modern web company does not need to have any batch data collection at all. The data a website generates is either activity data or database changes, both of which occur continuously. In fact, when you think about any business, the underlying mechanics are almost always a continuous process—events happen in real-time, as Jack Bauer would tell us. When data is collected in batches, it is almost always due to some manual step or lack of digitization, or it is a historical relic left over from the automation of some nondigital process. Transmitting and reacting to data used to be very slow when the mechanics involved transporting pieces of paper and humans did the processing. A first pass at automation always retains the form of the original process, so this often lingers long after the medium has changed.

Production "batch" processing jobs that run every day are often effectively mimicking a kind of continuous computation with a window size of one day. The underlying data is, of course, always changing.

This helps to clear up one common area of confusion about stream processing. It is commonly believed that certain kinds of processing cannot be done in a stream processing system and must be done in batch. A typical example I have heard used is computing percentiles, maximums, averages, or other summary statistics that require seeing all the data. But this somewhat confuses the issue. It is true that with computing, for example, the maximum is a *blocking* operation that requires seeing all the records in the window in order to choose the biggest record. This kind of computation can absolutely be carried out in a stream processing system. Indeed, if you look at the earliest academic literature on stream processing, virtually the first thing that is done is to give precise semantics to windowing so that blocking operations over the window are still possible.

Seen in this light, it is easy to share my view of stream processing, which is much more general: it has nothing to do with blocking versus nonblocking operations; it is just processing that includes a notion of time in the underlying data being processed and so does not require a static snapshot of the data on which to operate. This means that a stream processing system produces output at a user-controlled frequency instead of waiting for the "end" of the data set to be reached. In this sense, stream processing is a generalization of batch processing and, given the prevalence of real-time data, a very important generalization.

So why has the traditional view of stream processing been as a niche application? I think the biggest reason is that a lack of real-time data collection made continuous processing something of a theoretical concern.

Certainly I think the lack of real-time data collection is likely what doomed the commercial stream processing systems. Their customers were still doing file-oriented, daily batch processing for ETL and data integration. Companies building stream processing systems focused on providing processing engines to attach to real-time data streams, but it turned out that at the time very few people actually had real-time data streams. Actually, very early at my career at LinkedIn, a company tried to sell us a very cool stream processing system, but since all our data was collected in hourly files at that time, the only thing we could think to do with it was take the hourly files we collected and feed them into the stream system at the end of the hour! The engineers at the stream processing company noted that this was a fairly common problem. The exception actually proves the rule here: finance, the one domain where stream processing has met with some success, was exactly the area where real-time data streams were already the norm, and processing the data stream was the pressing concern.

Even in the presence of a healthy batch processing ecosystem, the actual applicability of stream processing as an infrastructure style is quite broad. It covers the gap in infrastructure between real-time request/response services and offline batch processing. For modern Internet companies, I think around 25 percent of their code falls into this category.

It turns out that the log solves some of the most critical technical problems in stream processing, which I'll describe, but the biggest problem that it solves is just making data available in real-time multisubscriber data feeds.

For those interested in more details on the relationship between logs and stream processing, we have open-sourced Samza (*http://samza.incubator.apache.org/*), a stream processing system explicitly built on many of these ideas. We describe many of these applications in more detail in the documentation (*http://bit.ly/samza-docs*). But this is not specific to a particular stream processing system, as all the major stream processing systems have some integration with Kafka to act as a log of data for them to process.

Data Flow Graphs

The most interesting aspect of stream processing has nothing to do with the internals of a stream processing system, but instead with how it extends our idea of what a data feed is from the earlier data integration discussion. We discussed primarily feeds or logs of *primary* data—that is, the events and rows of data directly produced in the execution of various applications. Stream processing allows us to also include feeds computed off of other feeds. These derived feeds look no different to consumers than the feeds of primary data from which they are computed (see Figure 3-2).

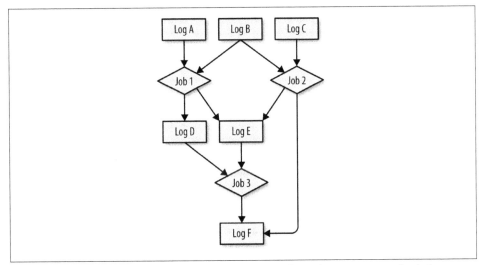

Figure 3-2. A multijob stream processing graph that flows data among multiple logs

These derived feeds can encapsulate arbitrary complexity and intelligence in the processing, so they can be quite valuable. For example, Google has described some details (*http://bit.ly/g-caffeine*) on how it rebuilt its web crawling, processing, and indexing pipeline—what has to be one of the most complex, largest scale data processing systems on the planet—on top of a stream processing system (*http://bit.ly/increment-pro*).

So what is stream processing? A stream processing job, for our purposes, will be anything that reads from logs and writes output to logs or other systems. The logs used for input and output connect these processes into a *graph* of processing stages. Using a centralized log in this fashion, you can view all the organization's data capture, transformation, and flow as just a series of logs and the processes that read from them and write to them.

A stream processor doesn't necessarily need to have a fancy framework at all; it can be any process or set of processes that read and write from logs. Additional infrastructure and support can be provided for helping manage and scale this kind of near-real-time processing code, and that is what stream processing frameworks do.

Logs and Stream Processing

Why do you need a log at all in stream processing? Why not have the processors communicate more directly using simple TCP or other lighter-weight messaging protocols? There are a couple of strong reasons to favor this model.

First, it makes each data set to be multisubscriber. Each stream processing input is available to any processor that wants it; and each output is available to anyone who needs it. This comes in handy not just for the production data flows, but also for debugging and monitoring stages in a complex data processing pipeline. Being able to quickly tap into an output stream and check its validity, compute some monitoring statistics, or even just see what the data looks like make development much more tractable.

The second use of the log is to ensure that order is maintained in the processing done by each consumer of data. Some event data might be only loosely ordered by time-stamp, but not everything is this way. Consider a stream of updates from a database. We might have a series of stream processing jobs that take this data and prepare it for indexing in a search index. If we process two updates to the same record out of order, we might end up with the wrong final result in our search index.

The final use of the log is arguably the most important, and that is to provide buffer-ing and isolation to the individual processes. If a processor produces output faster than its downstream consumer can keep up, we have three options:

- We can block the upstream job until the downstream job catches up (if using only TCP and no log, this is what would likely happen).
- We can just drop data on the floor.
- We can buffer data between the two processes.

Dropping data will be okay in a few areas, but is not generally acceptable, and is never really desirable.

Blocking sounds like an acceptable option at first, but in practice becomes a huge issue. Consider that what we want is not just to model the processing of a single application but to model the full data flow of the whole organization. This will inevi-tably be a very complex web of data flow between processors owned by different teams and run with different SLAs. In this complicated web of data processing, if any consumer fails or cannot keep up, upstream producers will block, and blocking will cascade up throughout the data-flow graph, grinding everything to a halt.

This leaves the only real option: buffering. The log acts as a very, very large buffer that allows the process to be restarted or fail without slowing down other parts of the processing graph. This means that a consumer can come down entirely for long peri-ods of time without impacting any of the upstream graph; as long as it is able to catch up when it restarts, everything else is unaffected.

This is not an uncommon pattern elsewhere. Big, complex MapReduce workflows use files to checkpoint and share their intermediate results. Big, complex SQL processing pipelines create lots and lots of intermediate or temporary tables. This just applies the pattern with an abstraction that is suitable for data in motion, namely a log.

Storm (*http://storm-project.net/*) and Samza (*http://samza.incubator.apache.org/*) are two stream processing systems built in this fashion, and can use Kafka or other similar systems as their log.

Reprocessing Data: The Lambda Architecture and an Alternative

An interesting application of this kind of log-oriented data modeling is the *Lambda Architecture*. This is an idea introduced by Nathan Marz, who wrote a widely read blog post describing an approach to combining stream processing with offline processing ("How to beat the CAP theorem" (*http://bit.ly/beat-cap*)). This has proven to be a surprisingly popular idea, with a dedicated website (*http://lambda-architecture.net*) and an upcoming book (*http://www.manning.com/marz/*).

What is a Lambda Architecture and How Do I Become One?

The Lambda Architecture looks something like Figure 3-3.

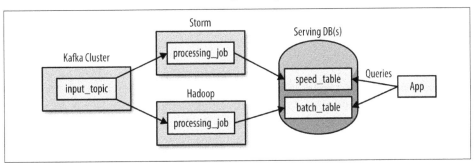

Figure 3-3. The Lambda Architecture

The way this works is that an immutable sequence of records is captured and fed into a batch-and-stream processing system in parallel. You implement your transformation logic twice, once in the batch system and once in the stream processing system. Then you stitch together the results from both at query time to produce a complete answer.

There are many variations on this, and I'm intentionally simplifying a bit. For example, you can swap in various similar systems for Kafka, Storm, and Hadoop, and people often use two different databases to store the output tables: one optimized for real-time and the other optimized for batch updates.

What's Good About This?

The Lambda Architecture emphasizes retaining the original input data unchanged. I think this is a really important aspect. The ability to operate on a complex data flow is greatly aided by the ability to see what inputs went in and what outputs came out.

I also like that this architecture highlights the problem of reprocessing data. Reprocessing is one of the key challenges of stream processing, but is very often ignored.

By "reprocessing," I mean processing input data over again to re-derive output. This is a completely obvious but often ignored requirement. Code will always change. So if you have code that derives output data from an input stream, whenever the code changes, you will need to recompute your output to see the effect of the change.

Why does code change? It may change because your application evolves and you want to compute new output fields that you didn't previously need. Or it may change because you found a bug and need to fix it. Regardless, when it does, you need to regenerate your output. I have found that many people who attempt to build real-time data processing systems don't put much thought into this problem and end up with a system that simply cannot evolve quickly because it has no convenient way to handle reprocessing.

And the Bad...

The problem with the Lambda Architecture is that maintaining code that needs to produce the same result in two complex distributed systems is exactly as painful as it seems it would be. I don't think this problem is fixable.

Distributed frameworks like Storm and Hadoop are complex to program. Inevitably, code ends up being specifically engineered towards the framework on which it runs. The resulting operational complexity of systems implementing the Lambda Architecture is the one thing that seems to be universally agreed on by everyone doing it.

One proposed approach to fixing this is to have a language or framework that abstracts over both the real-time and batch framework. You write your code using this higher-level framework and then it "compiles down" to stream processing or MapReduce under the covers. Summingbird (*http://bit.ly/summingbird*) is a framework that does this. This definitely makes things a little better, but I don't think it solves the problem. Ultimately, even if you can avoid coding your application twice, the operational burden of running and debugging two systems is going to be very high. Any new abstraction can only provide the features supported by the intersection of the two systems. Worse, committing to this new uber-framework walls off the rich ecosystem of tools and languages that makes Hadoop so powerful (Hive, Pig, Crunch, Cascading, Oozie, and so on).

By way of analogy, consider the notorious difficulties in making cross-database object-relational mapping (ORM) really transparent. And consider that this is just a matter of abstracting over very similar systems providing virtually identical capabilities with a (nearly) standardized interface language. The problem of abstracting over totally divergent programming paradigms built on top of barely stable distributed systems is much harder.

An Alternative

As someone who designs infrastructure, I think that the glaring question is this: why can't the stream processing system just be improved to really handle the full problem set in its target domain? Why do you need to glue on another system? Why can't you do both real-time processing and also handle the reprocessing when code changes? Stream processing systems already have a notion of parallelism, why not just handle reprocessing by increasing the parallelism and replaying history very quickly? The answer is that you can do this, and I think this is actually a reasonable alternative architecture if you are building this type of system today.

When I've discussed this with people, they sometimes tell me that stream processing feels inappropriate for high-throughput processing of historical data. This is an intuition based mostly on the limitations of systems they have used, which either scale poorly or can't save historical data. There is no reason this should be true. The fundamental abstraction in stream processing is data-flow DAGs, which are exactly the same underlying abstraction in a traditional data warehouse (such as Volcano (*http://bit.ly/volcano-ex*)), as well as being the fundamental abstraction in the MapReduce successor Tez (*http://hortonworks.com/hadoop/tez/*). Stream processing is just a generalization of this data-flow model that exposes checkpointing of intermediate results and continual output to the end user.

So how can we do the reprocessing directly from our stream processing job? My preferred approach is actually stupidly simple:

1. Use Kafka or some other system that will let you retain the full log of the data you want to be able to reprocess and that allows for multiple subscribers. For example, if you will want to reprocess up to 30 days of data, set your retention in Kafka to 30 days.
2. When you want to do the reprocessing, start a second instance of your stream processing job that starts processing from the beginning of the retained data, but direct this output data to a new output table.
3. When the second job has caught up, switch the application to read from the new table.
4. Stop the old version of the job and delete the old output table.

This architecture looks something like Figure 3-4.

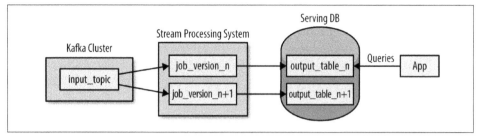

Figure 3-4. An alternative to the Lambda Architecture that removes the need for a batch system

Unlike the Lambda Architecture, in this approach you only do reprocessing when your processing code changes and you actually need to recompute your results. And of course the job doing the recomputation is just an improved version of the same code, running on the same framework, taking the same input data.

Naturally, you will want to bump up the parallelism on your reprocessing job so it completes very quickly.

Of course, you can optimize this further. In many cases you could combine the two output tables. However, I think there are some benefits to having both for a short period of time. This allows you to revert back instantaneously to the old logic by just having a button that redirects the application to the old table. And in cases that are particularly important (your ad targeting criteria, say), you can control the cutover with an automatic A/B test or bandit algorithm (*http://bit.ly/bandit-algorithms-optimization*) to ensure that whatever bug fix or code improvement you are rolling out hasn't accidentally degraded things in comparison to the prior version.

Note that this doesn't mean your data can't go to Hadoop, it just means that you don't run your reprocessing there. Kafka has good integration with Hadoop, so loading any Kafka topic is easy. It is often useful for the output or even intermediate streams from a stream processing job to be mirrored to Hadoop for analysis in tools such as Hive, or for use as input for other, offline data processing flows.

We have documented (*http://bit.ly/prev-data*) implementing this approach, as well as other variations on re-processing architectures using Samza.

The efficiency and resource trade-offs between the two approaches are somewhat of a wash. The Lambda Architecture requires running both reprocessing and live process-ing all the time, whereas what I have proposed only requires running the second copy of the job when you need reprocessing. However, my proposal requires temporarily having twice the storage space in the output database and requires a database that supports high-volume writes for the reload. In both cases, the extra load of the reprocessing would likely average out. If you had many such jobs, they wouldn't all reprocess at once, so on a shared cluster with several dozen such jobs you might budget an extra few percent of capacity for the few jobs that would be actively reprocessing at any given time.

The real advantage isn't about efficiency at all, but rather about allowing people to develop, test, debug, and operate their system on top of a single processing framework.

So in cases where simplicity is important, consider this approach as another option in addition to the Lambda Architecture.

Stateful Real-Time Processing

The relationship of logs to stream processing doesn't end with reprocessing. If the actual computations the stream processing system do require maintaining state, then that is yet another use for our good friend, the log.

Some real-time stream processing is just stateless record-at-a-time transformation, but many of the uses are more sophisticated counts, aggregations, or joins over windows in the stream. You might, for example, want to enrich an event stream (say a stream of clicks) with information about the user doing the click, in effect joining the click stream to the user account database. Invariably, this kind of processing ends up requiring some kind of state to be maintained by the processor; for example, when computing a count, you have the count so far to maintain. How can this kind of state be maintained correctly if the processors themselves can fail?

The simplest alternative would be to keep state in memory. However, if the process crashed, it would lose its intermediate state. If state is only maintained over a window, the process could just fall back to the point in the log where the window began. However, if one is doing a count over an hour, this might not be feasible.

An alternative is to simply store all state in a remote storage system and join over the network to that store. The problem with this is that there is no locality of data and lots of network round trips.

How can we support something like a table that is partitioned with our processing?

Well, recall the discussion of the duality of tables and logs. This gives us exactly the tool to be able to convert streams to tables colocated with our processing, as well as a mechanism for handling fault tolerance for these tables.

A stream processor can keep its state in a local table or index: a bdb (*http://bit.ly/oracle-berk-db*), RocksDB (*http://rocksdb.org/*), or even something more unusual such as a Lucene (*http://lucene.apache.org/*) or fastbit (*https://sdm.lbl.gov/fastbit*) index. The contents of this store are fed from its input streams (after first perhaps applying arbitrary transformation). It can journal out a changelog for this local index that it keeps to allow it to restore its state in the event of a crash and restart. This allows a generic mechanism for keeping co-partitioned states in arbitrary index types local with the incoming stream data.

When the process fails, it restores its index from the changelog. The log is the transformation of the local state into an incremental record-at-a-time backup.

This approach to state management has the elegant property that the state of the processors is also maintained as a log. We can think of this log just like we would the log of changes to a database table. In fact, the processors have something very like a co-partitioned table maintained along with them. Since this state is itself a log, other processors can subscribe to it. This can actually be quite useful in cases when the goal of the processing is to update a final state that is the natural output of the processing.

When combined with the logs coming out of databases for data integration purposes, the power of the log/table duality becomes clear. A changelog can be extracted from a database and indexed in different forms by various stream processors to join against event streams.

We give more detail on this style of managing stateful processing in Samza and many more practical examples (*http://bit.ly/samza-sm*).

Log Compaction

Of course, we can't hope to keep a complete log for all state changes for all time. Unless you want to use infinite space, somehow the log must be cleaned up. I'll talk a little about the implementation of this in Kafka to make it more concrete.

In Kafka, cleanup has two options depending on whether the data contains pure event data or keyed updates. By event data, I mean unrelated occurrences such as page views, clicks, or other things you would find in an application log. By keyed updates, I mean events that specifically record state changes in entities identified by some key. The changelog of a database is the prototypical example of this.

For event data, Kafka supports retaining a window of data. The window can be defined in terms of either time (days) or space (GBs), and most people just stick with the one week default retention. If you want infinite retention, just set this window to infinite and your data will never be thrown away.

For keyed data, however, a nice property of a *complete* log is that you can replay it to recreate the state of the source system. That is, if I have the log of changes, I can replay that log into a table in another database and recreate the state of the table at any point in time. This also works across different systems: you can replay a log of updates that originally went into a database into any other type of system that maintains data by primary key (a search index, a local store, and so on).

However, retaining the complete log will use more and more space as time goes by, and the replay will take longer and longer. Hence, in Kafka, we support a different type of retention aimed at supporting this use case, an example of which is shown in Figure 3-5. Instead of simply throwing away the old log entirely, we garbage-collect obsolete records from the tail of the log. Any record in the tail of the log that has a more recent update is eligible for this kind of cleanup. By doing this, we still guarantee that the log contains a complete backup of the source system, but now we can no longer recreate *all* previous states of the source system, only the more recent ones. We call this feature log compaction (*http://bit.ly/kafka-lc*).

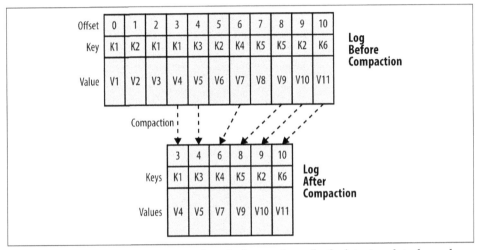

Figure 3-5. Log compaction ensures that the log retains only the latest update for each key. This is useful for modeling updates to mutable data as a log.

CHAPTER 4

Building Data Systems with Logs

The final topic I want to discuss is the role of the log in the internals of online data systems.

There is an analogy here between the role a log serves for data flow inside a distributed database and the role it serves for data integration in a larger organization. In both cases, it is responsible for data flow, consistency, and recovery. What, after all, is an organization if not a very complicated distributed data system?

Maybe if you squint a bit, you can see the whole of your organization's systems and data flows as a single very complicated distributed database. You can view all the individual query-oriented systems (Redis, SOLR, Hive tables, and so on) as just particular indexes on your data. You can view a stream processing system like Storm or Samza as just a very well-developed trigger-and-view materialization mechanism. Classical database people, I have noticed, like this view very much because it finally explains to them what on earth people are doing with all these different data systems—they are just different index types!

There is now undeniably an explosion of types of data systems, but in reality, this complexity has always existed. Even in the heyday of the relational database, organizations had many relational databases! So perhaps real integration hasn't existed since the mainframe when all the data really was in one place. There are many motivations for segregating data into multiple systems: scale, geography, security, and performance isolation are the most common. These issues can be addressed by a good system; for example, it is possible for an organization to have a single Hadoop cluster that contains all the data and serves a large and diverse constituency.

So there is already one possible simplification in the handling of data in the move to distributed systems: coalescing many little instances of each system into a few big clusters. Many systems aren't good enough to allow this yet because they don't have security, can't guarantee performance isolation, or just don't scale well enough. However, each of these problems is solvable. Instead of running many little single server instances of a system, you can instead run one big multitenant system shared by all the applications of an entire organization. This allows for huge efficiencies in management and utilization.

Unbundling?

My take is that the explosion of different systems is caused by the difficulty of building distributed data systems. By cutting back to a single query type or use case, each system is able to bring its scope down into the set of things that are feasible to build. Running all of these systems yields too much complexity.

I see three possible directions this could follow in the future.

The first possibility is a continuation of the status quo: the separation of systems remains more or less as it is for a good deal longer. This could happen either because the difficulty of distribution is too hard to overcome or because this specialization allows new levels of convenience and power for each system. As long as this remains true, the data integration problem will remain one of the most centrally important issues for the successful use of data. In this case, an external log that integrates data will be very important.

The second possibility is that there could be a reconsolidation in which a single system with enough generality starts to merge all the different functions back into a single uber-system. This uber-system could be superficially like the relational database, but its use in an organization would be far different, as you would need only one big system instead of umpteen little ones. In this world, there is no real data integration problem except what is solved inside this system. I think the practical difficulties of building such a system make this unlikely.

There is another possible outcome, though, which I actually find appealing as an engineer. One interesting facet of the new generation of data systems is that they are virtually all open source. Open source allows another possibility: data infrastructure could be unbundled into a collection of services and application-facing system API. You already see this happening to a certain extent in the Java stack:

- Zookeeper (*http://zookeeper.apache.org/*) handles much of the system coordination (perhaps with a bit of help from higher-level abstractions like Helix (*http://helix.incubator.apache.org/*) or Curator (*http://curator.incubator.apache.org/*)).
- Mesos (*http://mesos.apache.org/*) and YARN (*http://bit.ly/h-yarn*) process virtualization and resource management.
- Embedded libraries like Lucene (*http://lucene.apache.org/*), RocksDB (*https://rocksdb.org*), and LMDB (*http://symas.com/mdb*) do indexing.

- Netty (*http://netty.io/*), Jetty (*http://www.eclipse.org/jetty*), and higher-level wrappers like Finagle (*http://twitter.github.io/finagle*) and rest.li handle remote communication.
- Avro (*http://avro.apache.org/*), Protocol Buffers (*http://bit.ly/protobuf*), Thrift (*http://thrift.apache.org/*), and umpteen zillion (*http://bit.ly/jvm-serial*) other libraries handle serialization.
- Kafka (*http://kafka.apache.org/*) and BookKeeper (*http://bit.ly/a-bookk*) provide a backing log.

If you stack these things in a pile and squint a bit, it starts to look like a LEGO version of distributed data system engineering. You can piece these ingredients together to create a vast array of possible systems. This is clearly not a story relevant to end users who presumably care more about the API than about how it is implemented, but it might be a path towards getting the simplicity of the single system in a more diverse and modular world that continues to evolve. If the implementation time for a distributed system goes from years to weeks because reliable, flexible building blocks emerge, then the pressure to coalesce into a single monolithic system disappears.

The Place of the Log in System Architecture

A system that assumes that an external log is present allows the individual systems to relinquish much of their own complexity and rely on the shared log. Here are some things a log can do:

- Handle data consistency (whether eventual or immediate) by sequencing concurrent updates to nodes
- Provide data replication between nodes
- Provide "commit" semantics to the writer (such as acknowledging only when your write is guaranteed not to be lost)
- Provide the external data subscription feed from the system
- Provide the capability to restore failed replicas that lost their data or bootstrap new replicas
- Handle rebalancing of data between nodes

This is actually a substantial portion of what a distributed data system does. In fact, the majority of what is left over is related to the final client-facing query API and indexing strategy. This is exactly the part that should vary from system to system; for example, a full-text search query might need to query all partitions, whereas a query by primary key might only need to query a single node responsible for that key's data.

Here is how this works. The system is divided into two logical pieces: the log and the serving layer. The log captures the state changes in sequential order. The serving nodes store whatever index is required to serve queries (for example, a key-value store might have something like a btree or sstable, while a search system would have an inverted index). Writes can either go directly to the log, although they might be proxied by the serving layer. Writing to the log yields a logical timestamp (say the index in the log). If the system is partitioned, and I assume it is, then the log and the serving nodes will have the same number of partitions, even though they may have very different numbers of machines.

The serving nodes subscribe to the log and apply writes as quickly as possible to their local indexes in the order that the log has stored them (see Figure 4-1).

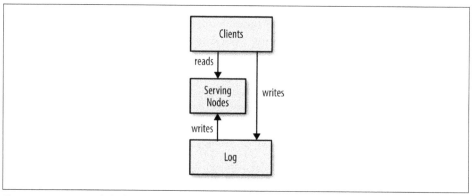

Figure 4-1. A simplified architecture for a log-centric data system

The client can get read-your-write semantics from any node by providing the timestamp of a write as part of its query. A serving node receiving such a query will compare the desired timestamp to its own index point, and if necessary, delay the request until it has indexed up to at least that time to avoid serving stale data.

The serving nodes may or may not need to have any notion of mastership or leader election. For many simple use cases, the serving nodes can be completely without leaders, since the log is the source of truth.

One of the trickier things a distributed system must do is handle restoring failed nodes or moving partitions from node to node. A typical approach would have the log retain only a fixed window of data and combine this with a snapshot of the data stored in the partition. It is equally possible for the log to retain a complete copy of data and compact the log itself (*http://bit.ly/kafka-lc*). This moves a significant amount of complexity out of the serving layer, which is system-specific, and into the log, which can be general purpose.

By having this log system, you get a fully developed subscription API for the contents of the data store that feeds ETL into other systems. In fact, many systems can share the same log while providing different indexes, as shown in Figure 4-2:

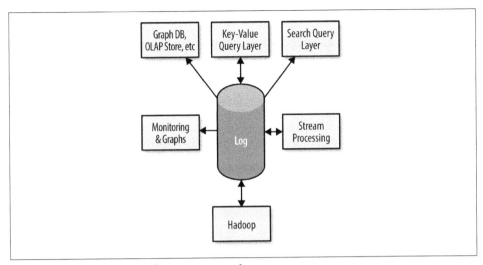

Figure 4-2. A log-centric infrastructure stack

Note how such a log-centric system is itself immediately a provider of data streams for processing and loading in other systems. Likewise, a stream processor can consume multiple input streams and then serve them via another system that indexes that output.

I find this view of systems as factored into a log and query API to be very revealing, as it lets you separate the query characteristics from the availability and consistency aspects of the system. I actually think this is even a useful way to mentally factor a system that isn't built this way to better understand it.

It's worth noting that although Kafka and BookKeeper are consistent logs, this is not a requirement. You could just as easily factor a Dynamo (*http://bit.ly/am-dynamo*)-like database into an eventually consistent AP log and a key-value serving layer. Such a log is a bit tricky to work with, as it will redeliver old messages and depends on the subscriber to handle this (much like Dynamo itself).

The idea of having a separate copy of data in the log (especially if it is a complete copy) strikes many people as wasteful. In reality, there are a few factors that make this less of an issue. First, the log can be a particularly efficient storage mechanism. We have the better part of a petabyte (PB) of log storage in Kafka in our live data-centers. Meanwhile, many serving systems require much more memory to serve data efficiently (text search, for example, is often all in memory). The serving system might also use optimized hardware. For example, most of our live data systems either serve out of memory or use SSDs. In contrast, the log system does only linear reads and writes, so it is quite happy using large multiterabyte hard drives. Finally, as shown in Figure 4-2, in the case where the data is served by multiple systems, the cost of the log is amortized over multiple indexes. This combination makes the expense of an external log fairly minimal.

This is exactly the pattern that LinkedIn has used to build out many of its own real-time query systems. These systems take as input either the log directly generated by database updates or else a log derived from other real-time processing, and provide a particular partitioning, indexing, and query capability on top of that data stream. This is how we have implemented our search, social graph, newsfeed, and OLAP query systems. In fact, it is quite common to have a single data feed (whether a live feed or a derived feed coming from Hadoop) replicated into multiple serving systems for live serving. This log-oriented data flow has proven to be an enormous simplifying assumption. None of these systems need to have an externally accessible write API at all; Kafka and databases are used as the system of record, and changes flow to the appropriate query systems through that log. Writes are handled locally by the nodes hosting a particular partition. These nodes blindly transcribe the feed provided by the log to their own store. A failed node can be restored by replaying the upstream log.

The degree to which these systems rely on the log varies. A fully reliant system could make use of the log for data partitioning, node restore, rebalancing, and all aspects of consistency and data propagation. In this setup, the actual serving tier is nothing less than a sort of cache structured to enable a particular type of processing, with writes going directly to the log.

Conclusion

Logs give us a principled way to model changing data as it cascades through a distributed system. This works just as well to model data flow in a large enterprise as it does for the internals of data flow in a distributed database. Having this kind of basic abstraction in place gives us a way of gluing together disparate data systems, processing real-time changes, as well as a being an interesting system and application architecture in its own right. In some sense, all of our systems are distributed systems now, so what was once a somewhat esoteric implementation detail of a distributed database is now a concept that is quite relevant to the modern software engineer.

References

If you made it this far you know most of what I know about logs; here are a few interesting references you may want to check out.

Everyone seems to use different terms for the same things, so it is a bit of a puzzle to connect the database literature to the distributed systems stuff to the various enterprise software camps to the open source world. Nonetheless, here are a few pointers.

Academic Papers, Systems, Talks, and Blogs

- These are good overviews of state machine (*http://bit.ly/cornell-sms*) and primary-backup (*http://bit.ly/pri-backup*) replication.
- PacificA (*http://bit.ly/pacific-a*) is a generic framework for implementing log-based distributed storage systems at Microsoft.
- Spanner (*http://bit.ly/g-spanner*)—Not everyone loves logical time for their logs. Google's new database tries to use physical time and models the uncertainty of clock drift directly by treating the timestamp as a range.
- Datanomic (*http://www.datomic.com/*): "Deconstructing the database" (*http://bit.ly/log-centric*) is a great presentation by Rich Hickey, the creator of Clojure, on his startup's database product.
- "A Survey of Rollback-Recovery Protocols in Message-Passing Systems (*http://bit.ly/rollback-survey*)"—I found this to be a very helpful introduction to fault tolerance and the practical application of logs to recovery outside databases.
- "The Reactive Manifesto" (*http://www.reactivemanifesto.org/*)—I'm actually not quite sure what is meant by reactive programming, but I think it means the same thing as "event driven." This link doesn't have much information, but this class (*http://bit.ly/principles-rp*) by Martin Odersky (of Scala fame) looks fascinating.

- Paxos!

  - Leslie Lamport has an interesting history (*http://bit.ly/l-lamport*) of how the algorithm was created in the 1980s but was not published until 1998 because the reviewers didn't like the Greek parable in the paper (*http://bit.ly/pt-parl*) and he didn't want to change it.
  - Once the original paper was published, it wasn't well understood. Lamport tried again (*http://bit.ly/simple-paxos*) and this time even included a few of the "uninteresting details," such as how to put his algorithm to use using actual computers. It is still not widely understood.
  - Fred Schneider (*http://bit.ly/fs-paxos*) and Butler Lampson (*http://bit.ly/bl-paxos*) each give a more detailed overview of applying Paxos in real systems.
  - A few Google engineers summarize their experience (*http://bit.ly/p-chubby*) with implementing Paxos in Chubby.
  - I actually found all of the Paxos papers pretty painful to understand but dutifully struggled through them. But you don't need to because this video (*http://bit.ly/paxos-lecture*) by John Ousterhout (*http://bit.ly/ousterhout*) (of log-structured filesystem fame) will make it all very simple. Somehow these consensus algorithms are much better presented by drawing them as the communication rounds unfold, rather than in a static presentation in a paper. Ironically, this video, which I consider the easiest overview of Paxos to understand, was created in an attempt to show that Paxos was hard to understand.
  - "Using Paxos to Build a Scalable Consistent Data Store" (*http://bit.ly/use-paxos*)—This is a cool paper on using a log to build a data store. Jun, one of the coauthors, is also one of the earliest engineers on Kafka.
- Paxos has competitors! Actually each of these map a lot more closely to the implementation of a log and are probably more suitable for practical implementation:

  - "Viewstamped Replication" (*http://bit.ly/viewstamped*) by Barbara Liskov is an early algorithm to directly model log replication.
  - Zab (*http://bit.ly/zab-pro*) is the algorithm used internally by Zookeeper.
  - RAFT (*http://bit.ly/raft-pro*) is an attempt at a more understandable consensus algorithm. The video presentation (*http://bit.ly/raft-lecture*), also by John Ousterhout, is great, too.
- You can see the role of the log in action in different real distributed databases:

  - PNUTS (*http://bit.ly/pnuts-sys*) is a system that attempts to apply the log-centric design of traditional distributed databases on a large scale.
  - HBase (*http://hbase.apache.org/*) and Bigtable (*http://bit.ly/bigtabl*) both give another example of logs in modern databases.
  - LinkedIn's own distributed database, Espresso (*http://bit.ly/li-ddsp*), like PNUTS, uses a log for replication, but takes a slightly different approach by using the underlying table itself as the source of the log.

- If you find yourself comparison shopping for a replication algorithm, this paper (*http://bit.ly/paxos-vs-zab*) might help you out.
- *Replication: Theory and Practice* (*http://bit.ly/rep-theory*) is a great book that collects a number of summary papers on replication in distributed systems. Many of the chapters are online (for example, 1 (*http://bit.ly/consist-m1*), 4 (*http://bit.ly/consist-m4*), 5 (*http://bit.ly/verita-5*), 6 (*http://bit.ly/history-6*), 7 (*http://bit.ly/vr-to-bft-7*), and 8 (*http://bit.ly/trust-survey-8*)).
- Stream processing. This is a bit too broad to summarize, but here are a few things I liked:
  - "Models and Issues in Data Stream Systems" (*http://bit.ly/models-issues*) is probably the best overview of the early research in this area.
  - "High-Availability Algorithms for Distributed Stream Processing" (*http://bit.ly/haa-dst*)
  - A couple of random systems papers:
    - "TelegraphCQ" (*http://bit.ly/telegraph-cq*)
    - "Aurora" (*http://bit.ly/vldb-aurora*)
    - "NiagaraCQ" (*http://bit.ly/niagara-cq*)
    - "Discretized Streams" (*http://bit.ly/hotcloud-ss*): This paper discusses Spark's streaming system.
    - "MillWheel: Fault-Tolerant Stream Processing at Internet Scale" (*http://bit.ly/mill-wheel*) describes one of Google's stream processing systems.
    - "Naiad: A Timely Dataflow System" (*http://bit.ly/naiad*)

Enterprise Software

The enterprise software world has similar problems but with different names.

Event sourcing
As far as I can tell, event sourcing (*http://bit.ly/fowler-es*) is basically a case of convergent evolution with state machine replication. It's interesting that the same idea would be invented again in such a different context. Event sourcing seems to focus on smaller, in-memory use cases that don't require partitioning. This approach to application development seems to combine the stream processing that occurs on the log of events with the application. Since this becomes pretty non-trivial when the processing is large enough to require data partitioning for scale, I focus on stream processing as a separate infrastructure primitive.

Change data capture
There is a small industry around getting data out of databases, and this is the most log-friendly style of database data extraction.

Enterprise application integration

This seems to be about solving the data integration problem when what you have is a collection of off-the-shelf enterprise software like CRM or supply-chain management software.

Complex event processing (CEP)

I'm fairly certain that nobody knows what this means or how it actually differs from stream processing. The difference seems to be that the focus is on unordered streams and on event filtering and detection rather than aggregation, but this, in my opinion is a distinction without a difference. Any system that is good at one should be good at the other.

Enterprise service bus

The enterprise service bus concept is very similar to some of the ideas I have described around data integration. This idea seems to have been moderately successful in enterprise software communities and is mostly unknown among web folks or the distributed data infrastructure crowd.

Open Source

There are almost too many open source systems to mention, but here are a few of them:

- Kafka (*http://kafka.apache.org/*) is the "log as a service" project that is the inspiration for much of this book.
- BookKeeper (*http://bit.ly/a-bookk*) and Hedwig (*http://bit.ly/apache-hedwig*) comprise another open source "log as a service." They seem to be more targeted at data system internals than at event data.
- Akka (*http://akka.io/*) is an actor framework for Scala. It has a module for persistence (*http://bit.ly/akka-persist*) that provides persistence and journaling. (There is even a Kafka plugin (*http://bit.ly/akka-github*) for persistence.)
- Samza (*http://samza.incubator.apache.org/*) is a stream processing framework we are working on at LinkedIn. It uses many of the ideas in this book, and integrates with Kafka as the underlying log.
- Storm (*http://storm.incubator.apache.org//*) is a popular stream processing framework that integrates well with Kafka.
- Spark Streaming (*http://bit.ly/sparkguide*) is a stream processing framework that is part of Spark (*http://spark.incubator.apache.org/*).
- Summingbird (*http://bit.ly/stream-mr*) is a layer on top of Storm or Hadoop that provides a convenient computing abstraction.

About the Author

Jay Kreps is a Principal Staff Engineer at LinkedIn where he is the lead architect for data infrastructure. He is the original author of several open source projects, including Voldemort, Kafka, Azkaban, and Samza.

Colophon

The animals on the cover of *I ♥ Logs* are gray-headed lovebirds (*Agapornis cana*). Also known as Madagascar lovebirds, these parrots are the only lovebird species that is not native to the African continent. They are also the smallest species of lovebird, and one of the most difficult to breed in captivity.

Adult female grey-headed lovebirds are entirely green; only the adult males have a gray upper chest and head. When fully grown, gray-headed lovebirds reach only about 5 inches long, and weigh just 30 grams. In the wild, these birds generally congregate in huge flocks to feed and find mates.

Although imported to Europe for aviculture in the late nineteenth century, few breeders have been successful in raising more than a generation or two of gray-headed lovebirds. This is largely due to the birds' intolerance of cold temperatures, which makes it hard for them to breed during the European autumn. Even the chicks that do manage to survive are not good pets, as they are generally too shy and nervous to accept humans as friends. Currently, there are strict export rules in place regarding these birds, making it very rare to find them outside of their native habitat.

The cover image is from Lydekker's *Royal Natural History*. The cover fonts are URW Typewriter and Guardian Sans. The text font is Adobe Minion Pro; the heading font is Adobe Myriad Condensed; and the code font is Dalton Maag's Ubuntu Mono.

Get even more for your money.

Join the O'Reilly Community, and register the O'Reilly books you own. It's free, and you'll get:

- $4.99 ebook upgrade offer
- 40% upgrade offer on O'Reilly print books
- Membership discounts on books and events
- Free lifetime updates to ebooks and videos
- Multiple ebook formats, DRM FREE
- Participation in the O'Reilly community
- Newsletters
- Account management
- 100% Satisfaction Guarantee

Signing up is easy:

1. Go to: oreilly.com/go/register
2. Create an O'Reilly login.
3. Provide your address.
4. Register your books.

Note: English-language books only

To order books online:
oreilly.com/store

For questions about products or an order:
orders@oreilly.com

To sign up to get topic-specific email announcements and/or news about upcoming books, conferences, special offers, and new technologies:
elists@oreilly.com

For technical questions about book content:
booktech@oreilly.com

To submit new book proposals to our editors:
proposals@oreilly.com

O'Reilly books are available in multiple DRM-free ebook formats. For more information:
oreilly.com/ebooks

Have it your way.

9 781491 909386